AF482691
TUMMY D

ONCE THERE WAS A LITTLE
SQUIRREL
WHOSE TAIL WAS FLUFFY, SOFT,
AND CURLED.

HIS NAME WAS TUMMY
D, HE LIVED UP HIGH IN
THE TALLEST TREE.
HE SLEPT AND ATE ALL
DAY LONG. TUMMY D
WAS A CHEEKY LAZY
SQUIRREL.

ONE DAY HE WOKE UP READY
TO DIG FOR FOOD. HE
SCAMPERED AND SCURRIED OVER
A LOG AND UNDER LEAVES.

LOOKING AND POKING,
SEARCHING FOR
SOMETHING TO EAT. HE
LOOKED AND LOOKED HE
EVEN CHECKED UNDER
SOME ROCKS.

HE DUG UNDER THE FLOWER LAYERS, BUT THERE WAS NOTHING LEFT, NOT EVEN A SCRAP.

UPSET, TUMMY D TRIPPED
ON A BIG ROCK.
HIS TAIL WAS DOWN,
MAKING HIM SLOW. HE
THOUGHT HE'S OUT OF
LUCK. THEN AGAIN,
TUMMY D READY TO GIVE
UP STUMBLED ON A PILE
OF MONKEY NUTS.

HE JUMPED UP AND DOWN
AND DANCED A LOT. HE ATE
SOME OF THE MONKEY
NUTS.

HE HIDES A FEW JUST AS A
THOUGHT ONE DAY HE MIGHT
RUN OUT OF LUCK. HE THEN GOT
BACK TO THE TREE AND
SNUGGLED UP FOR A NAP.

HUNGRY AGAIN,
TUMMY D WENT TO LOOK
FOR A SNACK.
HE RAN AND JUMPED AND RUN
SOME MORE.

ALL OF A SUDDEN, HIS FEET
WERE STUCK IN A TRAP, AND
THOUGHT HE WILL NEVER BE
ABLE TO WALK. CRYING FOR
HELP, BUT NO ONE COULD
HEAR HIM.

THEN TUMMY HEARD
SOMETHING STIRRING. HE
LOOKED STUNNED. HE
THOUGHT, THAT'S IT, MY END
IS HERE.

A FOX WAS COMING RUNNING
TOWARDS TUMMY D.
HE LOOKED PUZZLED.

TUMMY D AND WANDA

HOWEVER, WANDA WAS THE KINDEST FOX. ALL SHE EVER WANTED WAS TO HAVE A BFF.

SHE RAN TO HELP THE
LITTLE SQUIRREL. SHE
FREED TUMMY AND THEY
BECOME FRIENDS.

TIME PASSED BY AND TUMMY D
HELPED WANDA MAKE MORE
FRIENDS.
FROM THAT DAY ON, THEY
WERE THE BEST OF COMPANY.

WANDA GOT MORE THAN ONE
FRIEND, SHE GOT THE ENTIRE
FOREST TO THANK. FROM, THAT
DAY ON, SHE WASN'T ALONE
ANYMORE.

THE ANIMALS STARTED TO
HELP ONE ANOTHER.
AND THE FOREST BECAME A
PEACEFUL PLACE, LIKE NO
OTHER.

FOREVER AND AFTER, THEIR FRIENDSHIP LASTED. KINDNESS IS ALWAYS THE ANSWER.

I HOPE YOUR LITTLE
ONE ENJOYED TUMMY'S STORY.
LEAVE SOME MONKEY NUTS IN
YOUR BACKYARD AND MAYBE A
SQUIRREL WILL VISIT YOU TOO.